Communication Matters

31-Days to Speaking Life in Your Relationships

Communication Matters

This book is printed on acid-free paper.

Library of Congress Cataloging-in-Publication Data on file

ISBN 978-0-9907598-0-5

MANUFACTURED IN THE UNITED STATES OF AMERICA

Dedication
For Four Sisters
Jackie and Norma shaped me.
Nia and Kai stretch me.

Acknowledgements

This book was born out of another book project. The manuscript has been finished for years; but after multiple rejections and life transitions, it is yet to be published. However, I thank God for the "no's," for without them I would not be forced to dig deeper. Without them, I would not have developed new relationships.

My number one encourager is my husband, Harry. Save for me saying, "I think I want to go to the moon," I can always count on your response being, "OK. Let's make that happen." Thank you for always believing that I have something worthwhile to say and encouraging me to press forward.

A few years ago, I met Kathy Carlton Willis at a CLASSeminiar in St. Joseph, Missouri. She was supposed to be one of the leaders for my group, but she had injured her foot, so we did not get a chance to interact much. I was a published academic author, but I had never written a blog. Despite that, Kathy invited me to write for a blog for, about, and by pastors' wives. I nervously thought, *Certainly, I don't have something to say that others would find interesting.* I am so glad Kathy saw something that I did not. Thank you for generously sharing in the many ways you did and helping me develop my message. You helped to water the seed God had already placed in me.

I send a big shout-out to Johnny Stephens! Over the last few years, I have learned many things about the publishing industry, including the fact that it is a closed industry, few publishing houses are willing to take risks, and it is hard to get a personal response to much. However, for whatever reason, Johnny kept answering my calls; and because he did, I kept calling. When we talked, he took time (a lot of it) to talk to me. What started in 2009 with me trying to find a publisher for one project turned into something bigger. Thank you for every nugget of information shared; for helping me to think beyond one book, but rather developing a brand; and doing it so generously, graciously, and patiently.

Much love to my girls Nia and Kai. You both always take an interest in what Mommy is doing and speak life to me.

Table of Contents

Introduction

I knew I should have stopped talking, but I couldn't help myself. I had to have the last word. I had to prove I was right. I felt attacked. I had to defend my name, my integrity, and my honor—but, mostly, my pride.

Have you ever been in this situation? You knew if you kept talking, it would not lead to resolution but rather would only do more damage to the situation, whether it was with a spouse, a child, a family member, or a coworker.

Speaking life is an enormous challenge. Such a challenge applies to the person whose spouse has an idea that could possibly put a financial strain on the family finances. Or to the mother who is listening to her child tell her about a life-changing decision with which she disagrees. Or to the person who knows something derogatory about his coworker whose name has just come up in a conversation. We have daily opportunities to speak life, yet often we fail.

As Christians, we are called to use language that is forgiving, life-giving, and encouraging. A hallmark of our spiritual maturity is our ability to get along with others, and how well we communicate is a manifestation of that maturity. Often we fall short. We seek to be understood before we seek understanding. We offer correction to point out others' flaws and to boost our egos rather than to bring out the best in them. Sometimes we just talk too much. Consequently, we create barriers and damage our relationships. We cause confusion and chaos. Most importantly, we fail to glorify God in our speech.

We've all heard the phrase, "Communication is key"; but where do we learn to communicate? If we're lucky, we might take an elective in public speaking in high school. Rarely is there an interpersonal communication course required in elementary, middle, or high school. From whom do we learn to listen? Perhaps you saw good models of communication in your family; but even then, if your mother or father was good in math, you still had to take it every year in school.

Our society tells us that communication is key, but we often don't get formal training in it. Fortunately for believers, Scripture has much to teach us about speaking, listening, and other communication matters.

In this 31-day devotional, through the use of Scripture, daily challenges, and prayer, we are going work on getting rid of negative, unhealthy communication habits. We will examine matters of communication regarding our heart, mind, ears, and tongue. We can learn to say the right things, but our heart cannot mask our motives. What we say out of our mouth is reflective of what is in our heart and mind.

Before we speak, we should practice the art of listening. It is only through listening that we can gain understanding of other people's needs, feelings, perspectives, and motives. Wisdom is not gained through talking but rather listening; paying attention to our world and the people in it helps us to listen with an open ear.

Once our heart and mind are pure and we are open to listening, we can focus on our speech. Some things don't need to be said; others do. Words have power! Being aware of not only the choice of words we use but also how we say them can soften hearts, promote peace; lead to understanding and reconciliation; and, most of all, be pleasing to our Lord.

With each devotional, there is a daily challenge ("Reflect and Act") where we will take time to reflect on our current communication, a previous communication episode we could have handled better, or an action for the day.

Before we begin, ask the Lord to reveal areas in your heart and mind and in your listening and speech that are not pleasing to him. Ask him to reveal a relationship that needs attention; and throughout the next 31 days, be intentional about focusing on it. The other person does not have to know. This is between you and God.

Working on our heart and mind, practicing good listening skills, or being careful in the words we choose to say is a life-long process. In 31 days, you will not master effective communication in all areas of your life. However, my prayer is that we all will be more aware of our speech and the impact it has on another person, relationships, and situations. Hopefully, each of us can take with us a few biblical principles about effective communication that will have lasting impact.

Communication matters! Healthy, holistic communication does not just happen; we have to be intentional about creating it. Let us begin our journey together to speak life!

The Power
of the Spoken Word

Day 1

"And God said . . ." Genesis 1

The story of Creation is one of my favorite stories in the Bible. This story is powerful and demonstrates the awesomeness of God's character.

God spoke and created the cosmos and all of creation. From the beginning of creation, words had power. While we are not building the world, we are building our world with our words. Our words create our reality. Our words can speak things into existence—fear or love, doubt or confidence, distrust or security. We must respect the power of the spoken word.

Communication is more than speaking. It also includes listening and our attitudes and motives that influence our words.

God's character is inherently good and pure. Anything he speaks will also be good and pure. We, on the other hand, are not. We must be intentional about examining our heart, taking inventory of our mind, being observant about our speaking and listening habits, and making changes and adjustments where needed.

As we begin this 31-day journey, consider what changes you need to make in your heart, mind, listening, and speech.

Reflect and Act: Think of a time someone built you up with his or her words. How did that experience make you feel? How have you done the same to others? Think about a relationship in which you would like to improve the communication. List three ways you can do that.

Dear Lord, remind me today that my words have power. Remind me not to use them carelessly, frivolously, or thoughtlessly. Open my eyes to the areas of communication that need adjustments. Amen.

Reflection

Guard Your Heart

The Mouth Speaks What Is in the Heart

Day 2

"A good man brings good things out of good stored up in his heart and an evil man brings evil things out of the evil stored up in his heart. For the mouth speaks what the heart is full of." Luke 6:45

I doubt I could ever be a politician. Being all things to all people certainly has to be laborious. Sure, it's easy to have well-crafted positions, statements, and speeches, especially if you have a speechwriter. However, living what you say can be quite challenging.

During an election season, we can all think of times when a candidate's aspirations came to a screeching stop because he or she had a "slip of the tongue" that offended a particular demographic of people. We all make thoughtless mistakes in our speech. We have all said something before taking a moment to consider the implications of the comment.

Sometimes a slip of the tongue is unintentional, but at other times it can reveal what is in our heart. Our heart reveals our motives, our values, and who we are. It is hard to mask our heart for long. We might be able to do it for a little while, but eventually what is stored in our heart will come out of our mouth.

The heart doesn't lie. In 1 Corinthians 9:19-23, Paul wrote about being all things to all people to win souls for Christ;

but his heart, goals, and values were anchored in Christ, making it hard for him to speak with a double mind.

Before we can speak life, speak truth, or speak love, our heart has to be pure and filled with the right motives. That can only happen when we take an honest assessment of who we are and ensure that our heart is anchored in Christ and we desire to glorify Him in all that we think, say, and do. What is in your heart?

Reflect and Act: Examine your heart, and make a list of all the things in it. Are you often filled with pride, jealousy, bitterness, rage, or unforgiveness; or do you have the constant presence of love, joy, and peace?

Dear Lord, help me to see, with clarity, the things in my heart that are not pleasing to you. Show me the areas of my heart that need to be softened and that need to be more Spirit-filled and less flesh-filled. Convict me in the areas where I am blind. Teach me how to be different. Amen.

Reflection

Guard Your Heart

Day 3

"Above all else, guard your heart,
for it is the wellspring of life."
Proverbs 4:23

I take pride that I am not a gossip! There are some things I have heard about people (and I am not just talking about close family and friends) that I have never repeated and will probably take to my grave. I like to pat myself on the back about that. However, I have to be careful. While I haven't repeated things I have heard, I sure did like to know what was going on. I like to hear a good piece of juicy gossip as much as the next person, but I have to be intentional about starving that appetite.

Our heart is a wellspring, or a continuous supply of life-giving energy. It is our emotional, spiritual, and psychological center, guiding our thoughts, our speech and our behavior. It's not just what we let in our heart—gossip, stories in social media, or mindless television—it is also what we let fester—pride, anger, or past hurts. What we feast on is our wellspring of life. What we focus on gives us drive. What we thirst for quenches the desires of our heart.

We have to be careful who and what is allowed permanent residence in our heart. That which dwells in our heart shapes our values and determines what is important to us. The things we allow inside influence who we are and who we become.

Reflect and Act: Reflect on the state of your heart. What do you need to cultivate? What do you need to eliminate? How will you do both?

Dear Lord, reveal to me what I feast on, focus on, and crave in my heart. Show me the things, habits, and people I need to guard from entering my heart. Show me the heart qualities I need to eliminate and cultivate. Amen.

Reflection

A Pure Heart

Day 4

"He who loves a pure heart and whose speech is gracious will have the king for his friend." Proverbs 22:11

A few years ago, my friend Scott died. For those of us who knew and loved him, we would all say that he died much too young. Scott was an elder in his church and served in various capacities in law enforcement.

Two things stood out to me at Scott's funeral. First, the law enforcement community and those in his family, church, and community had the same testimony about the kind of person he was. Scott was a man of integrity; he loved the Lord; and he was consistent in who he was, no matter the context or the company.

Second, all those who spoke during his service talked about how he had the ability to make everyone he encountered feel important and special, regardless of rank, position, or lot in life. Scott could find humor in any situation and could use it to diffuse tension or redirect a conversation. He did it so smoothly, and you never noticed he was doing it intentionally. Scott made you feel affirmed. He was a good listener and made you feel as if what you had to say was important.

Scott was also gracious in his speech. He was an observer of human nature—strengths and flaws—but I never heard him speak maliciously about anyone. He had, what seemed to be, a natural ability to affirm people for who they were.

I left Scott's funeral knowing that was a skill I wanted to develop. I want people to say, "She makes me feel good when I talk to her." We can only do that when we have a pure heart.

A pure heart gives us a clearer lens through which to view the world, to help us see the positive in situations and people. A pure heart leads to gracious speech, which helps us to speak to others with kindness and gentleness, to affirm their humanity, and speak life into any situation. A pure heart and gracious speech attracts kings, whether superiors or subordinates. A pure heart and gracious speech also can turn enemies into friends.

Is your communication gracious? Does it draw people toward you, or does it turn them away?

Reflect and Act: As you reflect on your heart, be intentional about showing gracious speech to others today. Smile and hold the door open for someone. Ask someone how his or her day is, and listen. Greet someone in customer service (cashier or postal worker, for example) with genuine warmth. Make someone feel like he or she is the most important person in the world in that particular moment as you listen to him or her.

Dear Lord, continue to show me what is in my heart that is and is not pleasing to you. Show me how to cultivate a pure heart and eliminate those things that are not. Provide me opportunities today to demonstrate gracious speech to others. Amen.

Renew Your Mind

Renewing Your Mind

Day 5

"Do not conform any longer to the pattern of this world, but be transformed by the renewing of your mind. Then you will be able to test and approve what God's will is— his good, pleasing and perfect will." Romans 12:2

I've taught a course on interpersonal communication for a number of years. Without fail, when I get to the section about using "I-statements" instead of "you-statements," I inevitably have a few students who find that concept challenging because it makes them feel vulnerable. For example, instead of saying, "You are so rude and disrespectful," one would say, "When you use sarcasm when you talk to me, I feel belittled and hurt."

I-statements are challenging for most people, but I especially have found them to be challenging for the male students in my classes. Derek and Thomas were about 20 years old, athletes, and academically sharp. They read the textbook and participated in the lecture and class discussion. However, when it came time to rewrite you-statements and turn them into I-statements during a class activity, they refused. It was as if their brains would not let them do it.

Derek and Thomas found it difficult to even come up with I-statements. This challenge led to a long class discussion in which they declared, "These [statements] make you seem weak!"

Many of us are guilty of using you-statements most of the time and, like Derek and Thomas, are uncomfortable being vulnerable using I-statements. In order to learn new habits of communication, we have to renew our minds. We must reject the patterns of the world, which tell us "to get them before they get us," "look out for number one," or "don't take anything off anyone."

We conform to the pattern of the world when we respond in-kind instead of in-love, when we use sarcasm or passive-aggressive communication, and when we don't allow ourselves to be vulnerable without trusting our Father to protect us. Our natural, fleshly self perpetuates communication patterns of the world.

We cannot change these patterns by our own will; but with the help of our Father and the Holy Spirit, we can renew our minds to learn habits that are more productive, that cultivate healthy relationships, and that demonstrate love. Be purposeful in developing communication patterns that transform people; relationships; situations; and, ultimately, us.

Reflect and Act: What communication habit do you use that is not productive? What communication pattern do you use that would be acceptable to the world but not pleasing to the Father? Do you cut others off, use sarcasm, use passive-aggressive language, or put down others? Make a list of three things you can start or stop doing to improve your communication habits.

Dear Lord, help me to renew my mind so I can be open to learning new communication styles that glorify you. When I need to be vulnerable, help me not necessarily to trust the other person but to trust you. Reveal to me the communication behaviors I can begin or end today. Amen.

Think on These Things

Day 6

"Finally, brothers, whatever is true, whatever is noble, whatever is right, whatever is pure, whatever is lovely, whatever is admirable—if anything is excellent or praiseworthy— think about such things." Philippians 4:8

I met Sarah at a conference when we were graduate students. We saw one another every year at our professional convention, stayed in touch throughout the years, and became good friends when we were pregnant at the same time and shared the same due date. Now, when we attend our convention, we share a hotel room.

Sarah and I fight like sisters. Every year, I always leave, saying, "I'm going to get my own room next year!" I don't know if she thinks the same thing, but I am sure she leaves believing I am the epitome of an only child when it comes to sharing a room. Then, next year comes, and we share a room again.

A few years ago, Sarah met my college roommate, Jasmyn. Jas shared her stories about when we were students at Howard University. Sarah compared hers. The two women lamented about how difficult it is to share a room with me. I can't lie; it's true. I am a light sleeper. I am irritable when I am sleepy; and when I want to go to sleep, I want to go to sleep.

I jokingly told my friends that I felt like they were ganging up on me. They simultaneously said, "That is just you as a roommate. You are a great friend!" That made me feel good; but, more importantly, what they said was a teachable moment for me.

Just as my friends have done for me, I have had to learn how to compartmentalize other people's flaws. In the past, I had a tendency to write off someone if there was something about him or her I didn't like or that rubbed me the wrong way. "You are a conversational narcissist." "You are a lazy coworker who won't share the load." "You talk too much." I would roll my "internal eyes," put that person in a category, avoid him or her when I could, or write that person off all together if the offense was great enough.

Our challenge should be to focus what is right with people, not what is wrong. We all have flaws, but even the most obnoxious person has redeeming qualities, and we should focus on those things—thoughts that are pure, noble, right, true, lovely, and admirable.

When we think on "these things," it is easier for us to cultivate a habit of seeing the positive qualities of others. When we realize the grace God has shown us and how others accept us, it should be a reminder for us to stretch and do the same.

Reflect and Act: Think of someone who gets under your skin. Now consider his or her admirable qualities. If you have a loved one who has one characteristic that drives you crazy (for example, being late, indecisive, or lazy), instead of dwelling on his or her flaw, focus on the admirable qualities the person possesses.

Dear Lord, thank you for the grace you have given me. Help me to find, see, and value lovely, admirable, true, and pure things in others. If I tend to point out others' flaws, help me to now focus on their good qualities. Amen.

Is Your Heart and Mind Pleasing to the Lord?

Day 7

"I the LORD search the heart and examine the mind to reward a man according to his conduct, according to what his deed deserves." Jeremiah 17:10

Our hearts and mind are naturally inclined to sin. God already knows this because He created us. However, we try to fool ourselves, others, and even God as it relates to the condition of our heart and mind.

There is little we can do with our own might to change either. We can only make heart and mind changes when we surrender to the Lord by confessing where we are and trusting God to show us how to be different, even when we feel vulnerable to other people.

No one can shame us to be or do better; we have to want to be different. Ask the Lord to show you how, and be open to learning new ways of relating to others.

Reflect and Act: What has God revealed to you about the condition of your heart and mind? How does this condition affect how you communicate with others?

Dear Lord, thank you for new mercies and new opportunities to be different. Create in me a pure heart and a renewed mind so that my conversation is representative of you. Amen.

Reflection

Listen With an Open Ear

Don't Be a Fool

Day 8

"A fool finds no pleasure in understanding but delights in airing his own opinions." Proverbs 18:2

I come from a family where everyone has an opinion, and no one is shy about sharing it. I can recall gatherings with extended family where everyone talked at once, and he or she who talked loudest was heard. I learned then if you don't speak up—and sometimes loudly—your thoughts, opinions, and perspectives could be left out. So I learned to speak up.

Speaking up is not a bad characteristic. Speaking up has opened many doors for me. I've had the opportunity to create change when necessary and offer perspectives that others have not considered.

On the flip side, I could also be an opinion bully. I do have the gift of persuasion, but I can also continue to badger someone until they see that my opinion, perspective, or idea is the right, better, and logical one. No one could draw their line in the sand or dig in their heels better than me.

However, nothing can tame an opinion bully like marriage. Probably no other person has had a more profound impact on me being a better listener than my husband. I've had to work hard to be deliberate about listening. Early on in our marriage, I heard quite often, "That makes sense TO YOU." "There is more than one way to do it." "There is more than your perspective."

My strong and unyielding opinions grated on my husband. I quickly learned (well, maybe not quickly) that if I was going to stay married, I had to learn to listen. I had to consider other perspectives and other ways to do things. In order to do that, I had to listen.

Marriage helped me to be a better listener in other relationships as well. When I listened instead of sharing my opinions, I learned more about people; their motives; their understanding of the world; and, yes, other ways to approach a problem.

No matter if it is with your spouse, child, boss, sister, or coworker, it pays to listen. Do you spend more time trying to get others to see your point of view rather than understanding theirs? Proverbs 17:28 says, "Even a fool is thought wise if he keeps silent and discerning if he holds his tongue." Let's commit not to being a fool.

Reflect and Act: Today, just listen. Don't respond. If you do respond, ask the person more questions to gain clarity and understanding of his or her position or perspective. Only share your opinion when asked.

Dear Lord, help me not to be a fool. Help me not to delight in only sharing my opinions but rather listening to others. Help me to listen and be open to hearing new ideas and perspectives. When I think I will burst from not sharing my opinions, help me to contain myself. Teach me the discipline of only sharing my opinion or suggestion when asked. When I am not asked, even when I think my ideas are better, help me to keep it to myself. Amen.

Listening to Correction

Day 9

"He who listens to a life-giving rebuke will be at home among the wise." Proverbs 15:32

With impatience and annoyance, my husband once told me, "You are not on time for anything but work!" I took offense. Never mind me trying to understand him. I didn't like how he said it to me, and I didn't like what he said. Certainly, he was being unfair, and I was going to prove him wrong.

I am not late to everything. I am more of a "just in the nick of time" kind of girl. I am going to get somewhere right in time, but it takes a lot of unnecessary rushing without leaving time for the unexpected to happen. Well, OK, sometimes that does make me a few minutes late.

So, maybe he is right.

It's hard for me to admit this about myself because I see being on time as a virtue, a form of social and professional responsibility I perceive myself to embody. To admit this is to admit being flawed. I even debated about writing about this flaw of mine in this devotional.

Let's face it. It doesn't feel good to hear when we are wrong, come up short, or are just simply not perfect. Sometimes it is hard to accept criticism or correction. Our pride gets in the way; but the only way we can be wise and improve on being our best self is to listen to correction, even when it is not delivered in the most constructive manner. If the correction is delivered in a destructive way, we focus on the manner of the rebuke and not the content.

My husband and I have had many disputes that got off track

because of how something was said instead of concentrating on what was said. Even with this comment, he would probably admit that his goal was not to bring out the best in me but to communicate his frustration. However, even when the content stings, reminds us of our humanity and imperfection, or has an impure ulterior motive, we must be willing to listen to all correction.

When criticism and correction is presented in a negative manner or feels like an attack on your character, resist the temptation to defend yourself or focus on the attack. Instead, just listen. Figure out what you can learn as it relates to how you can be your best self, and leave the rest behind. As the saying goes, "Chew the meat and spit out the bone."

Reflect and Act: Think of a time when you rejected constructive criticism or correction. Consider if you should revisit this issue. If necessary, reach out to the person, and tell him or her you received it. Today, be open to receive correction without being defensive.

Dear Lord, help me not to be defensive when listening to correction and constructive criticism. When the correction is delivered in a nonconstructive way, help me to focus on what is of value, and show me what to leave behind. Amen.

Listen Before You Answer

Day 10

"To answer before listening—that is folly and shame."
Proverbs 18:13

Have you ever been guilty of waiting for someone to finish talking so you could express your point of view? While he or she was talking, you did not try to understand his or her perspective or feelings. You weren't seeking understanding with intentionality. Instead, you were just waiting—waiting for your turn to talk and get your point across. Worse, perhaps you didn't listen at all. Instead you loud-talked them or cut them off.

Listening is essential to healthy communication. We must first be purposeful about seeking understanding of the other person. Then, we can consider how to respond.

Finally, we speak. This trait sets the wise apart from the foolish.

Reflect and Act: Consider your conversational actions today. Do not cut others off when they are speaking. Reflect on what is being said to you before you answer. Be intentional about listening and not just hearing what others are saying.

Dear Lord, help me to be a better listener by being deliberate in gaining understanding for the other person's perspective. Help me not to cut off others, loud-talk them, or impatiently wait my turn to share my perspective. Help me to consider my response before I speak it. Provide an opportunity for me to exercise the discipline of listening. Amen.

Reflection

The Ears of the Wise Seek Knowledge

Day 11

"The heart of the discerning acquires knowledge, for the ears of the wise seek it out." Proverbs 18:15

For most of my life, I was a good student. I wasn't a natural straight-A student; but through a good work ethic and discipline, my mother helped me cultivate a love for learning. I was able to figure out what was required to get good grades. Consequently, I rarely needed to ask for help when it came to school.

However, that changed during the final leg of my doctoral program when it came time to write my dissertation. I was stuck. The task was so daunting it was too overwhelming to begin. I had writer's block. I became so immobilized I didn't touch it for about 18 months. I was defensive when someone asked me about it. I knew I had to finish, and the only way I could was to do something I normally shy away from doing. Ask for help.

I reached out to several people in my field whom I had met at conferences over the years. They were not formal mentors. Many of them had their own graduate students to direct and guide. However, to my surprise, each person I asked for help willingly agreed. They talked me through my ideas, read the first drafts of my proposal, and offered support and encouragement, all of which were enough to get me moving on the project.

After finally asking for help, it only took me nine months to complete the work. I never realized I had a problem asking for help until then. I didn't have a problem giving or offering help, but I sure did have one receiving it. There is something to be said for the lessons in self-sufficiency I was taught while I was growing up.

While we should take personal responsibility for our lives, we should seek wise counsel, especially when we don't have the answers. We should thirst for knowledge from God and from those He directs to us. I learned I have everything to gain when someone is willing to share knowledge with me. The only thing I have to lose is hearing someone say no, which puts me in no worse position than had I not asked for help.

Wisdom includes seeking out knowledge and understanding. To do this, we have to be intentional and active in our search.

Reflect and Act: Do you ask for help when you need it, or do you try to figure things out on your own? Why or why not? From whom do you ask for help or wise counsel? Identify a wise person, and ask him or her for a perspective or opinion.

Dear Lord, help me to be discerning in all situations. Show me through your Word and other godly sources where I can acquire knowledge. Amen.

Get the Facts!

Day 12

*"The first person to present his case seems right, until another
comes forward and questions him." Proverbs 18:17*

Many of us have had the experience of drawing conclusions that were wrong. We thought we saw, heard, and knew all there was to the situation. We thought we had the puzzle completed, but in reality we were missing a key piece. If we haven't been guilty of drawing conclusions, we have been the victim when one has drawn conclusions about us.

Before we speak, we need to get all the facts, even when the situation seems clear to us. When it comes to understanding people and their *modus operandi*, we must be aware that in some situations, we may never have all the facts. We may never have information about their life experiences that make them who they are. Therefore, always leave room to learn more about a story.

Reflect and Act: Reflect on a time you jumped to a conclusion. Consider how that episode or interaction could have been handled differently had you gathered all the facts.

Dear Lord, help me not to jump to conclusions. Help me to listen with discerning ears and ask questions that will lead to a more complete understanding. Amen.

Reflection

Overlooking Insults

Day 13

"A fool shows his annoyance at once, but a prudent man overlooks an insult." Proverbs 12:16

I have two daughters who are three and a half years apart. Sometimes they unintentionally offend one another. At other times, both of them are guilty of purposefully agitating the other.

When I am called to referee, I don't even have to ask what happened, because one of them, usually my older daughter, will have the look of guilty satisfaction that she has gotten a rise out of her sister. I tell both of them, to no avail, "If you just ignore your sister, she will move onto something else; but don't you see, she is trying to get a reaction from you."

How many of us are guilty because we have the need to respond when we hear an insult? We felt disrespected by a family member. A coworker used a passive-aggressive slight. A stranger cuts in front of us in the checkout line. A spouse brings an issue to your attention in a manner that is combative.

We have all heard things that offended us. There are times when we need to speak up, establish standards, and create understanding for how we should be treated. However, every slight or insult we hear does not need to be addressed.

Reflect and Act: Resolve not to let insults offend you. Consider a time when you did let an insult offend you. How could you have handled that experience differently?

Dear Lord, help me not to be offended easily. When I hear an insult, help me to let it roll off my back. Show me those times when

I need to speak up, and then give me the right words. Show me when I need to be quiet. Amen.

Reflection

What Kind of Listener Are You?

Day 14

"My dear brothers, take note of this: Everyone should be quick to listen, slow to speak and slow to become angry."
James 1:19

Listening is hard to do, especially when we don't feel heard. I know I get stuck on presenting my case, responding in anger, or harboring unforgiveness when I perceive another person is not listening or acknowledging my point of view or acknowledging their wrongdoing toward me.

However, the Bible is clear that we should be slow to respond as we consider our reply. Just because I think the other person doesn't hear me doesn't give me permission to talk louder, interrupt him or her, or just stop listening all together. In addition, we all can spend less time sharing our opinions and seeking to be understood rather than seeking understanding.

Ouch!

Seeking understanding rather than seeking to be understood is hard to do and takes spiritual maturity, discipline, and self-control. I don't know about you, but I am always in need of improving in this area.

Finally, we must be open to constructive criticism. Whether I don't like what is being said or how it is being said, I can always learn ways to be my best self when I am open to receiving correction and constructive feedback.

What kind of listener are you? Do you do the exact opposite of what James tells us to do? In what areas can you improve in order to listen with an open ear?

Reflect and Act: Find three people you trust, and ask them how you can improve your listening skills.

Dear Lord, show me how I can be a better listener. Help me to listen better to all people, especially those who are closest to me. Give me discernment and self-control. While I am learning to be a better listener with others, help me to listen more to you. Amen.

Reflection

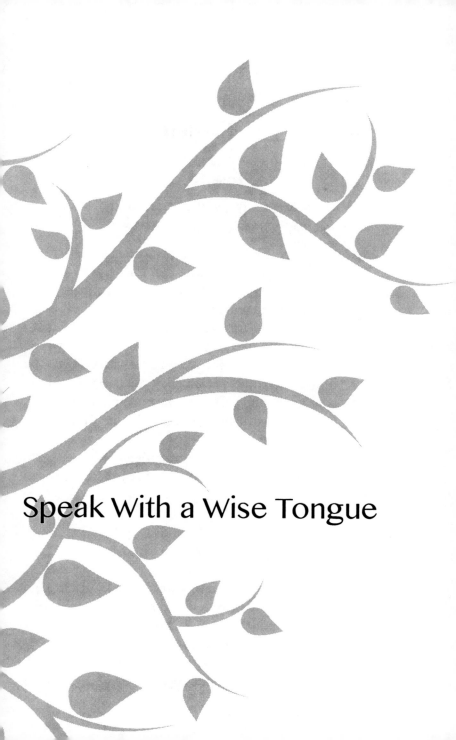

Speak With a Wise Tongue

Be Quiet!

Day 15

"When words are many, sin is not absent, but he who holds his tongue is wise." Proverbs 10:19

I came of age in the 1980s when hip hop music was clean and fun. One of my favorite groups was Run DMC, who sported shell-toe Adidas sneakers, rope chains, and Kangol hats. They rapped about the light-hearted aspects of life. Among their songs, one of my favorites, was "You Talk Too Much," a comical narrative of a young man they likened to the evening news and whose mouth was so big he could consume a Big Mac in one bite. The hook was, "You talk too much. / Homeboy you never shut up!"

Like many women, I love a good conversation, and there is nothing wrong with that. However, consider the times when we need to stop talking.

Is my timing appropriate? Your good friend has once again ended a short-lived relationship. Perhaps that moment is not the time to point out the poor choices she continues to make in choosing men.

Do I have all the facts? I once felt disrespected that a student continually came to my class late and then fell asleep. I defiantly pulled him up after class. It turned out that he worked third shift, got off work, and then was in class all day. I felt petty. If I had only had a conversation with him before I jumped to conclusions. It still doesn't excuse the behavior, but I didn't need to take it personally.

Is what I am saying necessary? What you have to say might be true, but it might not be nice or necessary. If your motive is not to bring the best out of people and situations, some things are best left unsaid. Either we are adding value, or we are taking it away. Words are never neutral.

Am I angry? There are many words that have been spoken in anger that have had long-lasting effects we regretted later.

So consider your timing, figure out if you have all the facts, discern whether your comments are necessary, and determine if you are speaking in anger. The more we talk, the more of an opportunity we have to be hurtful to others.

I've learned the hard way that every opinion does not need to be shared. Every nugget of information about another person does not need to be repeated—even if it is true. Every issue does not need to be addressed at the moment when we want to address it. Sometimes, it is just best to be quiet.

Reflect and Act: Consider the timing, truthfulness, necessity, emotion, and tone behind your words before you speak. If your comment is not true, necessary, or kind, don't share it. Think of a time when your comments did not add value to a situation. What happened?

Dear Lord, help me to be discerning with the words I choose to share. When I need to address an issue, show me the time to do it. When I have the opportunity to offer input, help me to remember to ask if it is true, nice, or even necessary. When I need to be quiet, help me to do that, too. Amen.

A Lying Tongue

Day 16

"The LORD detests lying lips, but he delights in men who are truthful." Proverbs 12:22

"I can't stand a liar!" These words are seared into my mind and memory from my mother. I could be many things, but a liar would not be one of them. When I was in high school, my mother caught me in a lie about how I got a ride home from a football game. She dropped my friend and me off at the game; and although I told her that my friend's mother would bring us home, instead, I rode home with a boy.

My friend and I planned in advance to ride home separately with the boys we were dating at the time. Unbeknownst to me, however, my friend was left stranded at the game. She thought I had left her on purpose, so she called my mother. When I arrived home and my mother asked, "Who brought you home?" I walked right into another lie.

My mother had preached to me my whole life how much she couldn't stand a liar. This incident was probably the first time I had lied. Thankfully, I wasn't good at it because I got caught the first time, too.

I knew I would get the punishment of a lifetime. I waited all weekend for something to happen. Instead, my mother said and did nothing as a consequence. Nothing. No long sermon. No punishment. No consequence. However, I felt so heavy and shamed; and I knew she was profoundly disappointed in me. I never lied to her again. Well, actually, I did, but I eventually would willingly confess my sins to her.

Like my mother, God detests a lying tongue. Lying violates the very foundation of any relationship. I, like my mother, have a low tolerance for lying; but I have learned that people usually lie out of fear. We, of course, fear consequences; but we also lie out of insecurity or lack of self-worth, to make ourselves look better.

While we are not necessarily lying to God directly, when we lie, we are basically saying we don't trust Him with our insecurities. We don't trust Him with our self-worth. We simply don't trust Him to be with us, even when we have to suffer consequences for our mistakes and rebellion.

Whether you tend to tell small fibs or you have a habit of telling big lies, trust God that He can be with you during the consequences or to work out your self-worth issues.

Reflect and Act: Think of a time you lied. Did it involve fear? doubt? insecurity? How did your lying reflect a lack of trust in God?

Dear Lord, help me not to having a lying tongue. Quench the spirit of rebellion in me where I do what I want because I want and then lie to avoid the consequences. Then help me to know that my self-worth and value come from you; and I don't have to lie to make myself look bigger, better, or more valuable. Help me to trust you in all situations. Amen.

Gossip

Day 17

"Without wood a fire goes out; without gossip a quarrel dies down." Proverbs 26:21

We live in a culture that thrives on an insatiable appetite for gossip about other people's affairs. None more evidenced than the many outlets for celebrity gossip as we talk about people and things that have no impact on our lives.

Gossip seems harmless because we don't personally know the people at the center of such news, but interest in the demise of others hits close to home, as well. We do celebrate the good news of others' new relationships, promotions, and personal accomplishments; but, if not checked, we can thrive on the drama of the break up, the showdown at the office, or the gross misconduct at the family reunion.

Just because you hear a juicy piece of gossip doesn't mean you have to pass it on. Our need to hear and share gossip says more about us than the people about whom we spend time talking. Gossip illustrates a need to feel better about ourselves, a need to be socially elevated because we are in the know, and a need to be self-righteous.

Before you repeat it, retweet it, or repost it, ask yourself what you will get out of playing the role of wood in a fire? Does this have a direct impact on you? Are you contributing to someone else's pain, embarrassment, or shame? Does your involvement help to resolve the issues?

Reflect and Act: Don't repeat anything negative that you hear. Consider a time when you played the role of the wood in a fire. How did it contribute to another person's pain, embarrassment, or shame? What did you get out of it?

Dear Lord, take away my desire to share or listen to gossip. Before another person in my presence can get started, help me to stop them in a spirit of love. Help me not to repeat or comment on it when I do hear it. Amen.

Reflection

Covering Offenses

Day 18

"He who covers an offense promotes love, but whoever repeats the matter separates close friends. " Proverbs 17:9

In general, my nature is to be forgiving. However, I can get stuck when the person who has wronged me does not acknowledge or apologize for an offense.

When we are wronged by someone, we might be tempted to tell others, who may or may not have anything to do with the issues at hand. Many of us have been guilty of finding someone to commiserate in our victimhood; or we might like to jockey for allies, people who will take our side, agree with us, and see how wrong the other party has done us.

"My sister owes me $100 and has the nerve to have purchased a new designer purse." "My ungrateful husband (or wife) doesn't appreciate me." "My coworker, once again, took credit for my idea." Unless you are sharing the offense with a person who can offer an unbiased perspective and can keep the matter confidential, think twice before you share. Instead address the issue with the person, and try to gain resolution.

Once the issue is resolved, leave it there. Do not repeat it; let the issue die. It is even harder to do when the person will not acknowledge or apologize for the offense. Keep quiet anyway. This is one way to demonstrate love.

Reflect and Act: Think about if and how you have been guilty of repeating offenses to others unnecessarily. If need be, go to a person who you believe has wronged you, and discuss the issue.

Dear Lord, help me address directly those with whom I have an issue and cover them in love by not repeating the offense to others unnecessarily. Amen.

Reflection

A Gentle Word

Day 19

"A gentle answer turns away wrath, but a harsh word stirs up anger." Proverbs 15:1

When we have been wronged, disrespected, or dismissed, we may feel justified to become loud or indignant with our response. When we take a stand for what is right, we rationalize fighting ugliness with ugliness.

A neighbor's dog continually poops in your yard, even though you've addressed the issue nicely with its owner. A customer sales representative was rude and dismissive to you. Your child responds in a way that is borderline disrespectful. "How dare he or she to talk to me like that!"

How will you respond? If you think about it, you don't like and probably don't respond well to harsh words. So why should we expect others to be different?

Set the example. A gentle answer doesn't mean you ignore the issue. You can still be firm in your position, but you will eliminate the automatic defensive response from the other person. Whether you are taking a stand for something that is morally and ethically wrong or responding to someone who has simply gotten under your skin, consider a gentle response today.

Reflect and Act: How do you normally respond when you believe you've been wronged, disrespected, or dismissed? Why do you respond that way? How could you respond differently?

Dear Lord, provide opportunities for me today to give a gentle answer. Help me not to respond with anger or annoyance, but rather give me the right words to diffuse and not intensify any tension. Amen.

Reflection

Building Up Others

Day 20

"Do not let any unwholesome talk come out of your mouths, but only what is helpful for the building others up according to their needs that it might benefit those who listen."
Ephesians 4:29

When I first started teaching nearly 20 years ago, I equated grading work with using a red pen to mark students' papers, telling them everything they had done wrong. That was the model I had experienced as a student, and I just repeated it.

Over time, I learned that that approach does little to help students produce their best work or to develop as critical thinkers, which is the goal of teaching. My job was to bring the best out of my students. That, too, should be our goal when we interact with our family members, coworkers, friends, and others.

We can only do that when we focus on what we share and how we share it. Everything we think doesn't always need to be said, even if it is true! We shouldn't avoid having difficult conversations. However, our goal should not be to get our way or to get the other person to see things our way. Instead, it should bring the best out of the person and the situation.

We are called to help build up others according to their needs. In our conversations, let's focus less on us and more on others.

Reflect and Act: Verbally build up and speak a word of encouragement to at least three people today.

Dear Lord, please provide an opportunity for me to encourage someone today. Give me the exact words they need. Amen.

Reflection

Nag Potential or Just a Nag?

Day 21

"Better to live in a desert than with a quarrelsome and nagging wife." Proverbs 21:19

I don't think my husband would call me a nag; but he certainly would say—and I would agree—I have nag potential. While I have grown in this area, I think to myself, *Hey, if you don't want me to be a nag, then do what I ask you to do the first time, then I only have to ask you once.*

After 16 years of marriage, two things stand out that have helped me curb my nag potential. First, I determine what is a need and what is a want. My husband once told me, "When everything is presented as a need, then we tend not to hear anything." There is a difference between wanting a cosmetic feature being fixed in a house and taking care of a leaking pipe.

It took me a while to learn the difference. My husband loves to do yard work. He enjoys it and takes pride in it. Unfortunately, his schedule is unpredictable, and he doesn't have a set day to work in the yard.

So once, after having asked my husband several times to manicure the overgrown bushes, I decided to shape them up myself. Mind you, I had never shaped bushes, cut grass, or anything of the like. I was a little scared to go back to the shed and get the "thing" to shape up the bushes (it looked like a good place for a North Carolina snake to hide); but I found it, figured out how to use it, and shaped up the bushes—pretty nicely I might add. Then I was sore for three days.

Once I let go of the desire to have the yard look a certain way, he decided, on his own, he needed to pay someone to take care of it. Wow! All I had to do was let it go. Now if he has some time, he will do it himself; otherwise, the yard man does it.

Second, letting go is important but so is praying. Some things I just need to take to the Lord and let He and my husband work it out. Like the yard work, I have found when I stop talking about something, something miraculous happens. The situation resolves itself without my help, as if God is telling me, "I got this, and I don't really need your help."

Imagine that. God doesn't need my help telling my husband what he needs or should do. Whether you are a spouse or a parent, commit to working to reduce your nag potential.

Reflect and Act: Consider how you feel when someone nags you. Why do you nag others? What do you want to accomplish? How can you decrease your nag potential?

Dear Lord, help me not be a nag. Give me discernment for when and how to bring up an issue. Help me to let go of things that are out of my control, and give me peace in doing that. Release my desire to control others. Amen.

Words That Bring Healing

Day 22

"Reckless words pierce like a sword, but the tongue brings wise healing." Proverbs 12:18

Though there are many benefits of social media and other forms of computer-mediated communication, one of the disadvantages is that people are more bold and rude than they would be in face-to-face communication. I found this to be true with some of my students, especially those who take my online classes.

I have received communication that left me thinking, *Seriously? I know you didn't just say!* I find this curious because the inappropriate and sometimes disrespectful communication was usually when a student wanted something, an extension or a grade renegotiation.

I have had to mature when responding to students who have said something I found offensive—mostly via e-mail. Of course, with mediated communication, we don't have the benefit of tone or other nonverbal cues. I try to be aware of that. I am also mindful that e-mail creates a record of communication.

With these things in mind, I try to model the communication I want to receive. I also know that I am communication-savvy enough to couch a nice "put-you-in-your place" comment tucked away in my professional, encouraging language. In order for me to continue to mature in this area, I knew I needed to leave those comments out.

Last semester, Tony was in my online class. Rarely did he follow the assignment directions; and then he would send me angry e-mails, demanding to know why he had received the grade that he had. In one e-mail, he even accused me of not liking him.

I won't lie. Tony did annoy me. However, I had to make a decision: Was I going to reply as sharply as I perceived him to be, or was I going to attempt to diffuse the tension existing between us? I chose the latter. I did not respond in kind, and I tried to focus on helping him be successful. Fortunately, my response paid off.

Finally, for the last two assignments, Tony stopped fighting me. He started reading the directions and taking my counsel. His e-mails were kinder. I have no idea if he was genuine or what motivated him to change his strategy of communication; but whatever it was, he and I were able to connect, and he was able to pass the class.

I have not mastered giving an apt reply, especially when I perceive the other person as offensive and disrespectful. I have to exercise much restraint and self-control; but for this test with Tony, at least, I think I passed. I am sure there will be more tests to come, and I continue to pray that I can tame my tongue and keystroke and use them to bring healing in a situation.

Reflect and Act: Think of a time when you tried a more gentle approach to change the direction of a conversation. Now, compare that to a time when you did not. Which had the better outcome?

Dear Lord, help me to use my words not as a weapon but instead to bring healing to an exchange. Amen.

Seasoned Speech

Day 23

"Let your conversation always be full of grace, seasoned with salt, so that you may know how to answer everyone."
Colossians 4:6

In the ancient world, salt was used for many things. This mineral was included in burnt offerings and sacrifices, and it could be a disinfectant as well as a seasoning. Salt also was and still is used as a preservative.

Our speech should be salty—tasty as well as preservative. When we use seasoned speech, what we say and how we say it is magnetic to others. Salty speech draws people closer; it does not repel them.

When our speech is seasoned with grace, we preserve relationships. Sharp, negative, snide, rude, judgmental, or sarcastic communication has little seasoning. That type of speech doesn't invite anyone for seconds. When our speech is full of love, forgiveness, and encouragement, we invite people for more.

Use your seasoned speech today.

Reflect and Act: Make an extra effort to have seasoned speech with at least three people today.

Dear Lord, help me to use my words so people can see Christ in me. Give me opportunities and the words today to invite people for seconds. Amen.

Reflection

Speak Up!

Day 24

"Speak up for those who cannot speak for themselves for the rights of all who are destitute. Speak up and judge fairly; defend the rights of the poor and needy." Proverbs 31:8-9

We live in a culture where it is easy to access information about others and acceptable to be preoccupied with someone else's business. On the flip side, when it matters, we can be guilty of not speaking up for what is right. You know something is unjust, unfair, and simply wrong, but it doesn't concern you or yours, so you keep your head down. Some of us are quick to speak up for ourselves but not so quick to do it for others.

Our 24-hour news cycle broadcasts corruption, injustice, oppression, and exploitation; and we have also become desensitized to it. We are commanded to speak up for those who cannot speak for themselves.

You might not be called to be a corporate whistleblower or go lead a march at the Department of Justice, but you can speak up for the person not present when their name is being dragged through the mud—if nothing else than to say, "Let's not talk about him in his absence." You can speak up for what's right in your community organization (church, PTA, Little League team) when you see that someone has been unfairly treated.

When you know for sure that an action, event, or words are contrary to the ways of God, speak up boldly.

Reflect and Act: When was a time that you should have spoken up but you didn't? Why not?

Dear Lord, give me the conviction, discernment, and wisdom to know when something is contrary to you, your ways, and your will. Give me the courage to be bold when I speak up for those who cannot speak for themselves. Amen.

Reflection

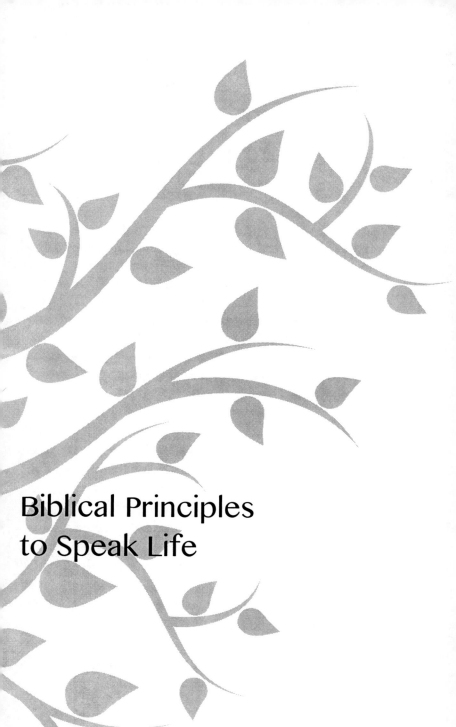

Biblical Principles
to Speak Life

Adam and Eve: Accepting Responsibility

Day 25

"But the Lord God called to the man, 'Where are you?' He answered, 'I heard you in the garden, and I was afraid because I was naked; so I hid.' And he said, 'who told you that you were naked? Have you eaten from the tree that I commanded you not to eat from? The man said, 'The woman you put here with me—she gave me some fruit from the tree, and I ate it." "Then the Lord God said to the woman, "What is this you have done?' The woman said, 'The serpent deceived me, and I ate it.' " Genesis 3:9-13

One day, my girls were bickering with one another so much they had worked my last nerve. I made them go to bed in their own rooms, with no electronics; but I asked them to write me a note telling why each could not get along with her sister and what she could do to have more self-control.

My younger daughter, who was 8 years old at the time, wrote, "I admit, I was bothering Nia; but that does not mean she wasn't bothering me." The line was comical to me. It also reminded me of my own reluctance to admit when I am wrong.

Like Adam and Eve, until we have matured, many of us avoid at all cost being accountable for our actions and words to others and to God. This is what we've inherited from the original sin. We don't want to admit our failures, our short-comings, our sinful, or selfish nature.

Unless there is a situation of abuse, rarely are we victims in our communication exchanges. We play a role in either diffusing or exacerbating the situation. We acknowledge our wrong-doing along with an excuse, explanation, or justification for our behavior. In order to cultivate healthy, whole communication, we must be real with ourselves and with God before we can do that with others.

The next time you need to acknowledge your shortcoming—"I was late. I am sorry." "I was tired, grumpy, and short, which is still no excuse. I am sorry"—remember to leave the *but* out of it, which is usually how we excuse our behavior. When we give an account to God for our words and actions, it is doubtful "the serpent made me do it" will be acceptable. No matter what others do or say to us, we are still accountable for our words.

Reflect and Act: Do you readily admit your shortcomings without justification, explanation, or excuse? Why do you think this is a challenge for you? How do you feel when others respond to your excuses?

Dear Lord, help me to admit when I am wrong without justifying my behavior. Help me to accept that being human means falling short. Also remind me that I have been forgiven of past sins and that I have victory to be better in Christ. Amen.

Abraham and Lot: Take the High Road in Resolving Conflict

Day 26

"Let's not have any quarreling between you and me, or between your herdsmen and me, for we are brothers. Is not the whole land before you? Let's part company. If you go left, I'll go to the right; if you go to the right, I'll go to the left." Genesis 13:8

There are times when we need to work hard and stretch to get along with others. There are also times we need to part ways.

Genesis 13 tells the story of Abraham and his nephew, Lot. God blessed their territory in such a way that the land could not support their cattle, herds, and herdsmen. The herdsmen bickered among themselves. Abraham's solution was to part ways.

As the patriarch of the family, Abraham was well within his right to choose the land he wanted first. Instead, he told Lot to make his choice, and he would go in the opposite direction.

Bickering, haggling, and fighting is like being a pig in mud; we can't get dirty with mud all the time as we stand our ground and demand what is rightfully ours. Sometimes we have to take the high road in resolving conflict.

In Genesis 12, God promises to make Abraham into a great nation. In the next chapter, Abraham does not take matters into his own hands. Abraham trusted God. Lot chose what appeared to be the best land for him. Even then, Abraham trusted God.

Do you trust God when you resolve conflict, or do you manipulate and scheme to make sure things work out in your favor? Next time, take the high road, and trust that God has your best interest, even if the other person does not.

Reflect and Act: How can you part ways, or distance yourself from a person or a group of people and still be amicable and genuinely concerned about their wellbeing?

Dear Lord, taking the high road is sometimes scary. I feel vulnerable and afraid others will not look out for my best interest. Help me to have more trust and faith in you than in my ability to stand my ground, to manipulate, or to scheme. Amen.

Reflection

Moses: Teach Me What To Say

Day 27

"Moses said to the Lord, 'O Lord, I have never been eloquent, neither in the past nor since you have spoken to your servant. I am slow of speech and tongue.' The Lord said to him, 'Who gave man his mouth? Is it not I, the Lord? Now go; I will help you speak and teach you what to say.' " Exodus 4:10-11

I remember when our first daughter was born, and my husband and I were attempting to put a playpen together that we bought to use at my mother's house. We almost had it completed, but there was a step we were missing. We referred to the manual (although it was unclear and of little help); and, finally, between the three of us, we figured out the missing step.

Fortunately for us, God's manual is clear. Whether you've been called to do something of Herculean size, like Moses, or you are trying to break generational communication habits, seek the Lord. He made us. He knows us. He knows what we need to achieve the goals he has set for us as well the tools we need to be different, to be better in our communication.

Reflect and Act: Name one thing you believe the Lord is calling you to do, but you have been avoiding it because you lack the confidence. Name one habit you want to break but don't know how.

Dear Lord, thank you for creating me the way you have. Please be an ever-present reminder that it's not self-confidence I need but God-confidence to accomplish any goal or create new ways of living. Amen.

Reflection

The 12 Israelite Spies: A Grasshopper Mentality

Day 28

"We seemed like grasshoppers in our own eyes, and we looked the same to them." Numbers 13:33

In Numbers 13:1, the Lord tells Moses to send men from each tribe to explore the land of Canaan, "which I am giving to the Israelites." The key word in this sentence is "giving." The Lord had already told the Israelites He was giving them the land; they just needed to explore it and report back to the tribes what they saw.

When the spies came back from scoping out the land, instead of focusing on the richness of it and all that was soon to be theirs, they focused on the people who were living there who were giants much bigger than the Israelites.

"I am giving you this land." The opinions, observations, and words of these ten men caused panic and rebellion among the entire 12 tribes of Israel. When we don't focus on the nature, character, promises, and might of God and instead of our own limitations, we too have a grasshopper mentality. We don't believe God and his power. We are afraid. We lower our expectations so we will be more prepared for defeat and disappointments.

Whatever the reason, we ultimately are saying we don't trust God. Whether our self-talk is in our head, spoken out loud, or to others, we make a difference in achieving and becoming all God has called us to be or living beneath our potential.

When it's time to think and dream big, are you always focusing on why it can't be done? With our own ability it probably can't be done. Next time, when you are engaged in negative self-talk, focus on the promises of God. "I am giving you this land."

Reflect and Act: What keeps you from experiencing the promises of God? What keeps you from thinking and dreaming bigger? What keeps you from making the dream a reality through action? When you are in doubt of what God has called you to do, do you focus on his promises, or do you engage in negative self-talk?

Dear Lord, teach me to know and focus on your character and promises. Help me to think and dream big. Convict me when negative self-talk comes out of my mouth. Help me to see the world, the task, and your people through your eyes. Amen.

Reflection

Caleb: Focus on the Positive—
Even When It Is Unpopular

Day 29

"Then Caleb silenced the people before Moses and said, 'We should go up and take possession of the land, for we can certainly do it.'" Numbers 13:30

Caleb was among the 12 spies sent to explore the land of Canaan. He had a different report than the other spies. He said, "Yes, we can!" Why was Caleb so confident? He focused on the promise of God in Numbers 13:1: "I am giving this land." To stand sure-footed among negativity speaks volumes of Caleb's character.

How many times have you caved to peer pressure or didn't speak up when you should have? We, too, can be like Caleb by getting all the facts, having the right attitude, and focusing on God's promises.

First, we need to we get the facts. There are times when God sends us to places sight unseen, and we do have to walk by faith. However, how awesome is our God that He told the Israelites to go survey the land and check it out for themselves? In essence, he was saying, "I am giving you this land," but gather the facts first.

We are called to walk by faith, but God always prepares us for the task. We have to have the right attitude. How easy it is to go with the crowd, especially when the majority is loud and negative. Our voice and opinion seem so small in comparison. Even when we are giving realistic assessments of situations, we can still focus on the positive. Most importantly, we can be prepared, and we can be positive; but if we don't focus on the promises of God, it is all in vain.

Caleb kept his eyes on God's promise: "I am giving you this land." Just as it was enough for Caleb, His promises are enough for us.

Reflect and Act: How can you be a positive person in the midst of negativity? What unpopular stances do you need to take despite others deeming you out of touch and illogical?

Dear Lord, thank you for always preparing me for the tasks you have called me to do. Help me to speak positively in all situations. Don't let me get sucked into negative conversation and energy of the crowd. When I am fearful or focus on my limited ability, remind me of your promises and help me to focus on those. Amen.

Reflection

Jesus: Defending Oneself

Day 30

"But Jesus made no reply, not even to a single charge—to the great amazement of the governor." Matthew 27:14

Early in my childhood, I was taught to defend myself. Most of us probably heard the school rule teachers told us: If someone hits you, tell a teacher. While I was told not to start fights, my mother made it clear that if someone hit me, I was to hit them back and then go tell the teacher. My mother assured me that while I might have to suffer the consequences at school, there would be none at home as long as I was defending myself.

My mother's philosophy was that people would continue to bully me until I stood up for myself. I can't say I disagree. I've carried that belief into adulthood. I had an experience as an adult where I believed a colleague was actively sabotaging me, primarily by discrediting me to our other colleagues. I felt the immediate need to do damage control and defend my name.

There are times when we do need to be active in preserving our reputation and name. There are other times we are just trying to preserve our ego and pride. What if we took the posture of Jesus during his trial before his crucifixion? If ever there was a person who had a right to defend himself, was Jesus, for he was innocent of all chargers. Yet he never made a reply to any charge.

We don't know why Jesus did not defend himself other than it fulfills the prophecy in Isaiah 53:7. Maybe he knew this was his mission that was to be carried out. Maybe he knew the people didn't want to hear the truth, so why bother? Whatever the case, the model Jesus provides should be our guide when we are only trying to preserve our image or ego.

Today, I am still learning that I don't have to hit first and then tell the teacher. I'm learning that I can just go tell my God; and he will show me how to fight the battle, even if it means being quiet.

Reflect and Act: What is your first reaction when you suspect you are being falsely accused or painted in an unflattering light? Have you ever considered letting something go? Why or why not?

Dear Lord, give me discernment to know when I should defend myself and when I should leave it to you. Help me to let go of pride and ego. Amen.

Reflection

Life-Giving Power

Day 31

"The tongue has the power of life and death and those who love it will eat its fruit." Proverbs 18:21

Words have power. In the beginning was the Word, and the Word was with God, and the Word was God. Words have power. Words can do ugly things. Words can create beauty. Words have power. By the word of the Lord, the heavens and earth were made and everything in it.

Words have power. Satan can plant a thought in our minds. We speak that thought. The illusion of that seed planted appears real. Words have power. With words, we can convince ourselves, and others to do great, unimaginable, and courageous things.

Words have power. With words, we can crush a spirit or dream. Words have power. With words, we can create a safe and loving home. With words we can create spaces of chaos, distrust, and discord.

Words have power. Our tongue is the instrument through which we speak life or death with our words. Careless tongues, untamed tongues, lying tongues, and boastful tongues lead to death.

Today, make a commitment to speak life with your words! Speak life with your hearts! Speak life with your minds! Speak life with your ears. Speak life with your tongues! Speak Life! Words have power.

Reflect and Act: Name three things you can do differently or better in examining your heart, renewing your mind, listening with an open ear, or speaking with a wise tongue?

Dear Lord, help me to create and cultivate a tongue that speaks life! Amen.

Reflection

CPSIA information can be obtained at www.ICGtesting.com
Printed in the USA
BVOW03s2117221014

371949BV00004B/62/P